Th
Bravest
Roman
of All

Leila Rasheed

Illustrated by **Fran Bueno**

OXFORD
UNIVERSITY PRESS

Ever since I was a child, I've loved ancient history, myths and legends. I grew up in Libya, where I was lucky enough to be able to explore the beautiful Greek and Roman ruins of Cyrene. Perhaps that's why the characters in Roman legend and history feel so alive to me. However, I only discovered the story of Cloelia when I was an adult. I hope you enjoy my retelling of this exciting legend about a brave Roman girl!

I have written several other books for children and teenagers, including *Empire's End*, an adventure for older readers, set in Roman Britain.

Leila Rasheed

Chapter One

Cloelia[1] was brave. Cloelia was fast. Cloelia was bold ...

For a girl!

Cloelia was the bravest. Cloelia was the fastest. Cloelia was the boldest ...

Of the girls!

Cloelia was fed up of hearing that last bit. She was a Roman after all, and all Romans were brave. Rome was only a little city, but the Romans had kicked out their cruel king, Tarquin, and recaptured their city by working together.

[1] (*say* Clo-ee-lee-a)

Cloelia remembered the day when the Romans defeated Tarquin and his gang. After the Romans threw him out, Tarquin had gone to get help from King Lars of the Etruscans. The Romans had woken one terrifying

King Lars

Etruscans

morning to find the Etruscan army outside their gates. The Etruscans wanted to charge into Rome and take over the city for Tarquin. But to do that, they had to cross the bridge over the river Tiber.

Rome

Romans

River Tiber

Luckily, Captain Horatio of Rome was ready to stop them. His Roman troops chopped through the legs of the bridge, so it collapsed before the Etruscans could cross. Horatio had been on the bridge, fighting back the Etruscans. He fell into the river when the bridge collapsed.

Cloelia had been watching from the city walls, like every other Roman. She had joined in the roar of victory when Captain Horatio surfaced in the river and swam to safety.

'No more kings for Rome!' the Romans shouted.

'No surrender! Rome forever!' Cloelia shouted along with everyone else. But the war was not over. The Etruscan army camped on a hill opposite Rome and stopped food from entering the city.

Chapter Two

Everyone liked Cloelia. Her laugh was the loudest, her grin was the cheekiest. Only her mother scolded her because her hair was always in a tangle from leaping over ditches or scrambling through bushes.

'Slow down, Cloelia,' said her mother. 'Walk like a lady, do your weaving, spinning, cooking and cleaning ... Cloelia! Come back here now!'

But no matter how high Cloelia climbed, or how far she leaped, or how many boys she beat at arm-wrestling, the boys still taunted her: 'You're pretty brave ... for a girl!'

'I'm not brave *for a girl* – I'm just brave!'
Cloelia protested. She sat with her big brother,
Marcus, on their garden wall, trying to ignore
her hunger. 'I'm as brave as any boy!'

'Look around you,' said Marcus, pointing to
the busy streets. 'All the warriors are boys.'

Cloelia looked at the Roman warriors. Some
of them were boys. Some of them were men.
They all looked scared sometimes.

'I could be a warrior,' said Cloelia. 'If they let
me have a spear.'

'Look at Captain Horatio! Do you really think you could be as brave as him?'

Cloelia looked at Captain Horatio as he rode past them on his fine black horse. He had looked terrified before he finally fell into the water on the day when he saved Rome.

'I could be a captain if they let me ride a horse!' Cloelia said.

Marcus burst out laughing. Only captains and the richest men were allowed to ride horses. The horses smelled sweet and their skin was as smooth as a petal in the sun. They snorted like the wind blowing in from the sea and their galloping hooves struck like lightning. Cloelia wanted to ride a horse more than anything. But no girl, no woman, had ever ridden a horse. Not in Rome.

'You'd fall off!' Marcus was still laughing.

Cloelia had seen the sons of the most important men having their riding lessons. Many of them had clung to their horse's manes and looked seasick.

'I might fall off the first time,' said Cloelia, 'but then I'd get back on.'

'You can't do those things. You're just a girl,' said Marcus crossly, jumping down from the wall. 'But don't worry, I'll save you from the Etruscan warriors.'

'One day *I* might save *you*,' said Cloelia.

But that night, Cloelia lay awake – and not just because she was hungry. She remembered her mother scolding her, and the boys teasing her. She wondered if she would ever get the chance to save anyone. *Maybe,* she thought sadly, *I will always be 'just a girl'.*

Chapter Three

One morning, Cloelia saw Etruscan messengers riding through the streets of Rome. They had come to talk, not fight. What would they say to Rome's leaders?

She soon found out. All the Romans were called to the Forum, the big square in the town centre, to hear the news.

'King Lars wants peace!' shouted Captain Horatio to the crowd. The Romans cheered, but when he spoke again, his voice was serious. 'But just to make sure we don't cheat, he wants forty children to go to the Etruscan camp as hostages.'

There was dead silence. Hostages could be sold as slaves, or even killed, if the peace did not last.

'We cannot refuse,' said Cloelia's father. He was not a warrior any more, but he was a powerful man who helped make the laws. 'But we must choose the children fairly – not like in the days of King Tarquin. All our children must pick a stone from this jar. There are forty white stones among the black stones. The forty children who draw the white stones must go as prisoners. No matter whose child they are.'

The sun beat down on Cloelia as she queued with the other children for her turn to choose a stone. Her mouth was dry and her stomach churned. *There are so many black stones*, she told herself. *Why would the one I pick be white?*

She reached the jar, put her hand in, and clenched her eyes shut as her fist closed around a stone.

She opened her hand. The stone was white. Now Cloelia didn't feel brave. What would happen to her beyond the walls of Rome, in the enemy camp? She wanted to cry.

Marcus's lip was wobbling, and she saw that he was holding a white stone, too.

I can't choose my fate, Cloelia thought, *but I can choose how I behave. I can cry and scream ... or I can be brave. Maybe if I'm brave, Marcus will be brave too.*

She marched up to her father and the other leaders. Her father's face fell as she held out her hand with the stone in it.

'I am ready,' she said loudly, so all the Romans could hear her.

* * *

She had not been ready for the ropes around her wrists. She was King Lars's prisoner now. The boys were chained together and guarded by twenty Etruscan soldiers. The girls were guarded by just one soldier, who rode alongside them sleepily. After all, they didn't think *girls* would dare to run away!

It was a long march to the Etruscan camp.
Some of the smallest children were crying, so
the older ones carried them. Cloelia's legs were
tired and aching by the time they reached the
Etruscan camp.

They entered the camp: a circle of tents pitched closely together. Cloelia smelled stew cooking over a fire. The Etruscan soldiers marched the children into the shade and made them sit down. The boys were kept chained up and guarded, but the girls were untied and left alone. A young soldier brought them water. Then Cloelia's stomach rumbled loudly, so he brought them some stew as well.

Cloelia glanced around nervously as she ate. Where was King Lars? She couldn't see anyone who looked like a king.

All she could hear was birdsong, the wind flapping the cloth tents, and the scrunch-scrunch of the soldiers' horses munching the grass. All she could see were men with tired eyes cleaning their armour and clothes, rubbing down the horses, or simply sleeping. *Why are they so relaxed?* she wondered. Then she realized. It had been so easy to take hostages that they thought they had won.

'King Tarquin!' gasped a girl next to her. Cloelia looked up sharply. The other children shuddered as he came riding over to them, his golden crown gleaming, his purple cloak as bright as blood.

'So these are the Roman prisoners,' he said
with a sneer. 'Your leaders said they would never
surrender, but now we have their children!'

The children huddled together. Cloelia's
cheeks burned.

'We are not *your* prisoners,' she said. 'We are the hostages of King Lars!'

'Say another word and you will regret it,' snapped Tarquin. Cloelia knew she had to be silent.

King Tarquin rode away.

'How dare he speak to us like that!' began one of the girls, and others agreed, but in low voices. They all feared King Tarquin.

'How long will they keep us here?' someone asked. No one knew. But now everyone was frightened, and Cloelia was angry too.

Some of the older girls began telling cheerful stories to the youngest ones. Cloelia had never been good at looking after little children. Instead, she looked around her. She remembered sitting on her father's knee years ago, as he told Marcus how to plan an attack, drawing lines in the dust with a stick.

'Spot the weak points,' he had said. 'Make a plan.'

Now Cloelia spotted a bare patch where a
tent had once been pitched. It made a gap in
the wall of the camp – a weak spot. A soldier
stood in the gap, his spear tall next to him like
a twin brother, but his eyes were sleepy, and
he yawned. Just beyond him, the river Tiber
gleamed, coiled like a protective snake around
the hills of Rome.

I could run, thought Cloelia. *I can swim. I could escape across the river.* She was the fastest, the strongest, the bravest of the girls ... but what about the others? To run without them would not be brave, it would just be running away. Even though it made escape so much harder and more dangerous, she had to take them with her – if they would come. Quickly, she shared her plan with them.

The girls looked scared.

'They'll catch us,' said one, shaking her head hard. 'We'll be killed.'

'What about the boys?' asked another.

Cloelia looked over at the boys' group. The toughest-looking soldiers stood near them.

'We can't rescue them,' she said, 'but we can save ourselves at least.'

'I can't walk anymore,' piped up a little girl tearfully. 'My feet hurt.'

Cloelia was silent. Then she saw a large white horse. As it grazed, it had drifted away from the other horses. It twitched its tail to shake off the flies, and the way it stamped its hoof and shook its mane told her it was full of energy.

'I have an idea,' Cloelia whispered to the other girls. 'I'll free that horse and we'll drive it into the camp. While the soldiers are chasing it, we'll steal the other horses and ride them down to the river!'

'Ride?' The girls stared at her with wide eyes. 'But girls don't ride.'

'We do now,' said Cloelia firmly.

Chapter Four

They waited until evening, when the sunset made the shadows long and the soldiers were eating around the campfire. Cloelia took a pin from her dress and crept over to the white horse. 'Sorry, horse,' she murmured. Then she pricked its leg with the sharp pin.

The horse gave a startled neigh and bolted.
The soldiers shouted in alarm and ran after
it, dropping their food. Cloelia and the older
girls raced through the shadows, shooing
the younger girls ahead of them. When they
reached the other horses, Cloelia helped the
younger girls to climb on.

'Follow me!' Cloelia whispered. She ran, pulling the horses after her. The horses, startled, began trotting and then – spooked by the unfamiliar riders on their backs – broke into a gallop. Cloelia stumbled as the horses she had been leading suddenly overtook her. Hooves thudded into the hard ground and sent mud flying up, stinging her face like wasps. She caught her balance and kept running, terrified by the angry shouts from the Etruscan soldiers. Never had she run faster!

The horses were far ahead of her now, the girls on their backs bumping up and down like sacks of clothes. Cloelia's heart hammered. She heard hissing all around her – hissss thwack! Hissss thwack! – and suddenly there were long sticks growing out of the ground.

Not sticks, she realized in terror. *Spears!* The Etruscans were hurling spears after them.

Now the ground sloped steeply down to the river. Cloelia leaped – never had she leaped further! – and splashed down into the cold Tiber. She found her feet, spitting out river water. All around her, girls jumped down from the horses and swam or waded across the river, carrying the smaller ones. At last, they reached the other side. Roman soldiers came running down to the river. They stared in disbelief, then leaped into action, pulling the girls from the water.

Cloelia grabbed the strong hand a Roman soldier reached out to her, and she was hauled up onto the bank. She glanced behind her. The Etruscans were lined up on the opposite shore of the Tiber, yelling angrily and shaking their spears. As the Roman soldiers pulled the girls into the walls of the city and bolted the great gates behind them, Cloelia thought she was safe at last.

She was wrong.

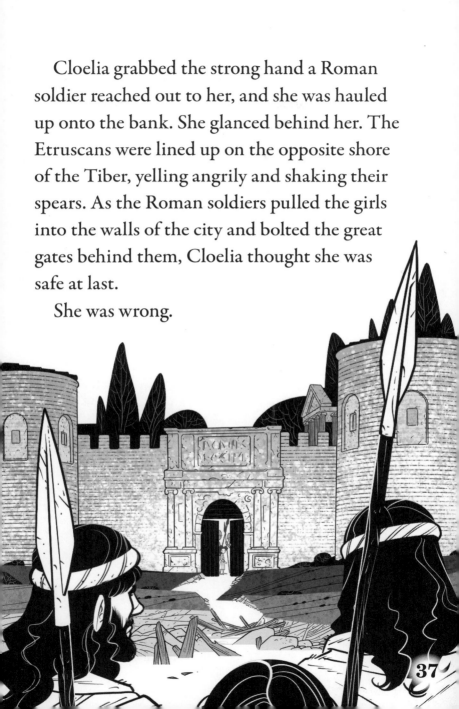

Chapter Five

'Whose idea was it to escape?' Captain Horatio's furious voice boomed out across the forum the next morning. The city leaders watched the girls, their faces stern as stone.

There was dead silence. Cloelia slowly raised her trembling hand. Her stomach felt as if she had swallowed not just river water, but cold jumping frogs and slimy wriggling fish.

'Cloelia. I might have known!' Her father rose to his feet, towering above her. 'Daughter, you have brought shame on the city and endangered us all.'

'But—'

'Enough! King Lars accuses us of breaking the peace treaty. He wants the leader of the girls sent back – none of the others.' He sighed and his voice softened a little. 'We were close to making peace. You should have trusted us.'

Cloelia hung her head. As the soldiers led her away, one of the girls ran up to her.

'Please see if my brother is OK,' she begged. 'He should have come home instead of me … he's only little.'

'I'll try,' said Cloelia.

'Thank you! You're the bravest Roman I know,' she whispered, and squeezed Cloelia's hand before she ran back into the crowd.

But am I? thought Cloelia. *Maybe I am just the silliest.*

She was still hanging her head when she was marched out of the city a few hours later, by Romans this time. They handed her over to grim-faced Etruscan soldiers.

'King Lars himself wants to see you,' one of them said gruffly. 'That was *his* horse you drove into the camp, and it took us hours to catch it.'

Cloelia felt sick. *I've been a fool,* she thought.
She would have been treated well if she had
stayed obediently in the camp as a hostage.
Now, King Lars himself was furious with her,
and would probably punish her horribly. At
least, she thought, she had managed to free the
other girls. That was the only shred of comfort
she had. The walk to the Etruscan camp was
even harder the second time.

* * *

The boys watched her fearfully as she was marched into the camp. Marcus caught her eye and gave her a grin. 'So brave,' he mouthed, and she could see the admiration in his eyes. It did not cheer her up, though. She was too frightened of what would happen when she finally met the monstrous King Lars.

Most of the horses had been caught again, and they were in pens – except for King Lars's horse. That was being held by a soldier, near three men who were sitting on small folding stools. There were two older men with greying hair, and one younger one who was writing on a scroll.

Cloelia realized that one of these men must be King Lars, but she could not tell which. She looked for the purple cloak, golden rings and crown that King Tarquin wore. But all three of these men were dressed like Etruscan soldiers, in light armour and a rough woollen cloak to keep off the wind.

Her gaze flicked nervously from man to
man, but none of them showed they were a
king, raging and bullying as King Tarquin
had. At least you knew to get out of Tarquin's
way. *This* king was like a scorpion, hiding in
the rocks.

'So this is the famous Cloelia! What possessed you to cause such chaos?' It was only when he spoke that Cloelia realized: the young man, writing on the scroll, was King Lars himself. It startled her so much that she replied, proudly and loudly, without thinking of manners.

'If you had attacked my city, I would have fought to the death before I let you take me as a prisoner. We came in peace, but Tarquin treated us as if he had captured us in battle.'

The older men looked at King Lars. He frowned.

'I did not like the way King Tarquin behaved,' he admitted. 'Kings should come to the aid of other kings, but I have had enough of Tarquin's cruel bullying. The Romans should not be forced to accept a king they hate. But that does not change what you did.'

He got to his feet and Cloelia winced, waiting for him to announce her punishment.

'Not only did you escape, but you saved the other girls,' King Lars said. 'That was a brave action, worthy of a king. I respect you, Cloelia, and I will free you and give you any gift you may wish for.'

Cloelia was too amazed to speak.

'Th-thank you,' she finally managed to say.

'What gift do you want?' King Lars asked. 'Gold? Jewels? Land?'

Cloelia turned to the group of hostages. She met Marcus's eyes.

'Please let me take the boys home with me,' she said. 'They are children too – and their parents are missing them.'

King Lars nodded. 'I thought you might say that. I agree. This war is over. I don't want to be the enemy of a city with such brave people. You and the hostages are free to go. Please honour me by accepting this gift for yourself.'

The soldier stepped forward and handed the rope to Cloelia. She looked up at the king's horse in disbelief.

'For me?'

'For you, to ride.'

'But girls don't ride,' she gasped.

King Lars smiled. He stepped forward and offered his hand to help her mount the horse.

'This girl has earned it,' he said.

* * *

'No more kings for Rome!' The cheers rang out as Cloelia rode back to the gates of Rome, with the boys she had saved walking behind her. All along the walls, men shook their spears and cheered.

'Hooray for Cloelia! Hooray for King Lars!' Mothers held their children high in the air to see their heroine. Rich men threw gold at Cloelia's feet as she rode, blushing and smiling, through the streets.

'Rome forever! Cloelia forever!'

Five hundred years later, little Rome had grown large enough to swallow the hill where King Lars once camped. Now the Forum was bigger, and it was surrounded by statues of great Roman men, riding horses. But one of the statues was of a great Roman girl. When she lived, she was the bravest, the fastest, the boldest of all the Romans … and her name was Cloelia.

Historical Note

Rome wasn't always an empire. When Rome was first founded, it was a small city ruled by kings. These kings were not always good people, and Tarquin was one of the worst. The Romans decided to throw him out and rule themselves instead. However, Lars and the other kings around Rome were worried about this. What if their subjects got the same idea? King Lars joined Tarquin in trying to take Rome back.

But the Romans – with the help of heroes like Captain Horatio and Cloelia – impressed King Lars with their bravery and determination to be independent. King Lars gave up trying to attack Rome and became their ally instead. King Tarquin, with no support and no army, gave up and went far away.

This history, and the story of Cloelia (circa 506 BCE), was written down by a Roman historian called Livy, hundreds of years after it was supposed to have happened. Cloelia may have been a legend, like King Arthur, but she was a legend that every Roman knew. Other Roman heroines are praised for being dutiful wives and good mothers. Cloelia is the only Roman heroine we know about who was famous for 'virtus', the Romans' word for bravery and independence. Of course, in real life there were probably lots of brave, independent girls like Cloelia, just as there are today.

Cloelia's statue was placed at the top of the Sacred Way, the most important road in Rome, which shows that Romans were proud of her. Her statue showed her riding a horse, and no other female was given this honour in Ancient Rome.